Farm animals

Katie Daynes
Designed by Nickey Butler and
Catherine-Anne MacKinnon

Illustrations by Christyan Fox

Farm animals consultant: David Uren
Reading consultant: Alison Kelly,
Roehampton University

Contents

On the farm

Sheep, hens and cows live on farms but so do other animals such as ostriches and fish.

Farmers keep animals for their milk, eggs, meat, skin, feathers or wool.

People and farms

All over the world, people build farms so they can keep their animals close by.

Long ago, animals only lived in the wild. People hunted them for meat.

Then, people learned to fence in the animals they hunted.

They found that the animals' eggs, wool and milk were useful too.

Today, some farm animals live in huts.

Others live in big open fields.

Farmers grow fields of grass for their sheep and cows to eat.

Feeding time

Farm animals can't always find things to eat. Farmers give them extra food and drink.

Farmers feed their sheep hay when snow covers the grass.

Newborn chicks are given trays of grain and water.

After a week, they learn to eat grain from a feeder.

They get water by tapping their beaks on a drinker.

Grass is tough to eat. Cows swallow it once, then bring it back into their mouth to chew again. This is called chewing the cud.

On a ranch

Ranches are farms with lots of land. On beef ranches, farmers breed cattle for their meat.

In spring, the ranchers herd their cattle to the hills where there's lots of grass to eat.

Before the cold winter, ranchers round up the cattle and herd them back to the farm.

On very big ranches, helicopters round up the cattle.

The noise of the helicopter makes the cattle move forward.

To catch an animal, a rancher throws a lasso over its horns.

Laying eggs

Female chickens are called hens. All hens lay eggs but only some eggs hatch into chicks.

Some farmers keep hens for their eggs.

Each day, fresh eggs are taken and sold.

For an egg to hatch into a chick, a male chicken has to mate with a hen.

Male chickens are called cockerels or roosters.

1. After a cockerel and hen have mated, the hen makes a nest.

2. She lays some eggs and sits down to warm them.

3. She uses her beak and feet to turn the eggs over.

4. After 21 days, a chick hatches out of each egg.

Chickens that are allowed to run around outside are called free-range chickens.

11

Milking

Cows, goats and sheep are often kept by farmers for their milk.

Several days after a cow gives birth, it goes with the other cows to be milked.

A milking machine is attached to the cows' teats. Their milk goes into a tank.

The cows are milked twice a day. Their milk is collected by a milk tanker.

Many farmers milk their animals by hand. They squeeze a teat and the milk squirts into a bowl.

Some farmers play music while their sheep are milking. It makes the sheep produce more milk.

Shearing

Sheep don't need their thick woolly coats in summer. Farmers shear them off and the wool is used to make clothes and blankets.

Sheepdogs help farmers round up sheep on hillsides.

Some farmers tell their sheepdogs what to do by blowing a whistle.

The sheep are herded into a pen.

Their wool is sheared off in one piece.

Then the farmer lets the sheep go.

Alpacas are also kept on farms. They have very soft wool.

These Alpacas have just been sheared.

Pigs and piglets

Pigs are often muddy, but they keep their huts dry and clean.

They search for food on the ground. Farmers give them food pellets to eat.

To keep cool, pigs roll in wet mud.

Then they stretch out and let the mud dry.

Pigs have a very good sense of smell. They can be trained to sniff out rare mushrooms.

Baby pigs are called piglets. A mother pig can give birth to 14 piglets at a time.

Lambs and calves

When farm animals are born, their mothers look after them. Often the farmer helps too.

A farmer helps a sheep give birth.

The mother gets up and licks her lamb.

The lamb can stand up after a few minutes.

Lambs are marked with paint to show which mother they belong to.

Teat

Mother cows usually have one calf.
The calf sucks milk from its mother's teat.

Baby lambs know who their mother is
because she makes her own bleating noise.

Ducks and geese

Ducks and geese are farmed for their eggs, feathers and meat.

This farmer is taking his ducks to a market to sell.

Geese live in groups. A group of geese is called a gaggle.

Some geese and ducks can't be trusted to sit on their own eggs until they hatch.

A farmer takes a freshly laid egg from a goose's nest.

She puts it into a hen's nest and the hen keeps it warm.

21

Underwater farms

Sometimes fish are kept on farms. Salmon farmers breed salmon in freshwater tanks. Then they take them to a farm in the sea.

The fish live in big pens made of netting. A walkway floats between the pens.

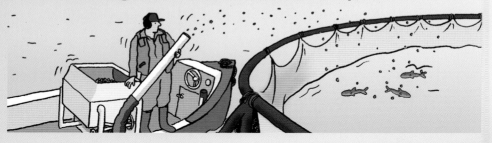

The farmer arrives at the salmon farm by boat. He sprays food pellets into the pens.

On some underwater farms, pearls are grown inside shellfish called oysters.

The salmon pens are checked by a diver.

He looks out for holes and dead fish.

After 18 months in their pens, the salmon are big enough to be caught and sold.

Big birds

Farmers breed ostriches for their eggs, skin and meat. Their feathers are used to make fancy clothes and hats.

They are kept in big fields so they have space to run.

To move an ostrich, the farmer puts a hood on its head.

Darkness calms the bird. Now the farmer can move it.

Ostrich chicks live together in a pen.
The farmer gives them food pellets to eat.

One ostrich egg makes an omelette big enough to feed 12 people.

Snow and sand

Only a few kinds of farm animals live in very cold or very hot places.

In some cold countries, reindeer are farmed for their meat, milk and skin.

Some reindeer farmers use snowmobiles to round up their animals.

In hot deserts, farmers camp where there is food for their animals.

When there are no more plants to eat, the farmers move their animals on.

Farmers who travel with their animals are called nomads.

Crocodile farms

Farmers breed crocodiles mostly for their skins, but also for their meat.

Crocodiles need to be kept in a warm place with water.

Some crocodiles are as long as three tall men lying down in a line.

1. A crocodile builds a nest with her feet.

2. She lays about 50 eggs in the nest.

3. Farmers put the eggs in an incubator to keep them warm.

4. After 80 days, baby crocodiles hatch out of the eggs.

Glossary of farm words

Here are some of the words in this book you might not know. This page tells you what they mean.

 hay - dried grass. Farmers feed hay to their cows and sheep in winter.

 breed - to keep and look after animals and their babies.

 cattle - a general word used to talk about cows and bulls.

 teat - the place where milk comes out of a cow, sheep, camel or goat.

 shear - to cut off the wool of a sheep, alpaca or other animal.

 nomads - farmers who travel with their animals to find food.

 incubator - a heated box where eggs can be kept until they hatch.

Websites to visit

You can visit exciting websites to find out more about farm animals.

To visit these websites, go to the Usborne Quicklinks website at **www.usborne.com/quicklinks**
Read the internet safety guidelines, and then type the keywords "**beginners farm animals**".

The websites are regularly reviewed and the links in Usborne Quicklinks are updated. However, Usborne Publishing is not responsible, and does not accept liability, for the content or availability of any website other than its own. We recommend that children are supervised while on the internet.

This Highland calf lives in the mountains of Scotland. Its thick coat protects it from the cold, windy weather.

Index

Acknowledgements

Cover design: Michelle Lawrence and Zoe Wray
Photographic manipulation: John Russell and Emma Julings

Photo credits

The publishers are grateful to the following for permission to reproduce material:
Agripicture.com 4-5, 6, 18; © **Alamy Images** (Elmar Krenkel/Corbis Bridge)1, (Robert Harding Picture Library Ltd) 20, (Jan Baks) 25; © **Alvey & Towers** 2-3; © **Bruce Coleman** (Jens Rydell) 28-29; © **CORBIS** (David R. Stoecklein) 8-9, (Don Mason) 10, (Bernard and Catherine Desjeux) 13 & 27, (Charles Philip) 14, (Dave G. Houser) 15, (George McCarthy) 16, (Tom Stewart) 17, (Niall Benvie) 31; © **Digital Vision** 21; © **FLPA** **(Foto Natura Stock)** 22-23; © **Getty Images** (Harvey Lloyd) 24, (Wayne R Bilenduke) 26; © **National Geographic Stock** (Stephen St. John) 19; © **Photoshot** (Joe Blossom) cover

Every effort has been made to trace and acknowledge ownership of copyright. If any rights have been omitted, the publishers offer to rectify this in any subsequent editions following notification.

With thanks to

Susan Smith at White House ostrich farm, Hartley's Creek crocodile farm